The Key Facts™ on

Uzbekistan

Essential Information on Uzbekistan

By Patrick W. Nee

The Internationalist®

www.internationalist.com

I0494179

The Internationalist®

International Business, Investment, and Travel

Published by:

The Internationalist Publishing Company

96 Walter Street/ Suite 200

Boston, MA 02131, USA

Tel: 617-354-7722

www.internationalist.com

PN@internationalist.com

Table Of Contents

Chapter 1: Background

Russia conquered the territory of present-day Uzbekistan in the late 19th century. Stiff resistance to the Red Army after the Bolshevik Revolution was eventually suppressed and a socialist republic established in 1924. During the Soviet era, intensive production of "white gold" (cotton) and grain led to overuse of agrochemicals and the depletion of water supplies, which have left the land degraded and the Aral Sea and certain rivers half dry. Independent since 1991, the country has lessened its dependence on the cotton monoculture by diversifying agricultural production while developing its mineral and petroleum export capacity and increasing its manufacturing base. However, longserving septuagenarian President Islom KARIMOV, who rose through the ranks of the Soviet-era State Planning Committee (Gosplan), remains wedded to the concepts of a command economy, creating a challenging environment for foreign investment. Current concerns include post-KARIMOV succession, terrorism by Islamic militants, economic stagnation, and the curtailment of human rights and democratization.

Chapter 2: Geography

Location:

Central Asia, north of Turkmenistan, south of Kazakhstan

Geographic coordinates:

41 00 N, 64 00 E

Map references:

Asia

Area:

total: 447,400 sq km

country comparison to the world: 57

land: 425,400 sq km

water: 22,000 sq km

Area - comparative:

slightly larger than California

Land boundaries:

total: 6,221 km

border countries: Afghanistan 137 km, Kazakhstan 2,203 km, Kyrgyzstan 1,099 km, Tajikistan 1,161 km, Turkmenistan 1,621 km

Coastline:

0 km (doubly landlocked); note - Uzbekistan includes the southern portion of the Aral Sea with a 420 km shoreline

Maritime claims:

none (doubly landlocked)

Climate:

mostly midlatitude desert, long, hot summers, mild winters; semiarid grassland in east

Terrain:

mostly flat-to-rolling sandy desert with dunes; broad, flat intensely irrigated river valleys along course of Amu Darya, Syr Darya (Sirdaryo), and Zarafshon; Fergana Valley in east surrounded by mountainous Tajikistan and Kyrgyzstan; shrinking Aral Sea in west

Elevation extremes:

lowest point: Sariqamish Kuli -12 m

highest point: Adelunga Toghi 4,301 m

Natural resources:

natural gas, petroleum, coal, gold, uranium, silver, copper, lead and zinc, tungsten, molybdenum

Land use:

arable land: 9.61%

permanent crops: 0.8%

other: 89.58% (2011)

Irrigated land:

41,980 sq km (2005)

Total renewable water resources:

48.87 cu km (2011)

Freshwater withdrawal (domestic/industrial/agricultural):

total: 56 cu km/yr (7%/3%/90%)

per capita: 2,113 cu m/yr (2005)

Natural hazards:

NA

Environment - current issues:

shrinkage of the Aral Sea has resulted in growing concentrations of chemical pesticides and natural salts; these substances are then blown from the increasingly exposed lake bed and contribute to desertification and respiratory health problems; water pollution from industrial wastes and the heavy use of fertilizers and pesticides is the cause of many human health disorders; increasing soil salination; soil contamination from buried nuclear processing and agricultural chemicals, including DDT

Environment - international agreements:

party to: Biodiversity, Climate Change, Climate Change-Kyoto Protocol, Desertification, Endangered Species, Environmental Modification, Hazardous Wastes, Ozone Layer Protection, Wetlands

signed, but not ratified: none of the selected agreements

Geography - note:

along with Liechtenstein, one of the only two doubly landlocked countries in the world

Chapter 3: People and Society

Nationality:

noun: Uzbekistani

adjective: Uzbekistani

Ethnic groups:

Uzbek 80%, Russian 5.5%, Tajik 5%, Kazakh 3%, Karakalpak 2.5%, Tatar 1.5%, other 2.5% (1996 est.)

Languages:

Uzbek (official) 74.3%, Russian 14.2%, Tajik 4.4%, other 7.1%

Religions:

Muslim 88% (mostly Sunni), Eastern Orthodox 9%, other 3%

Population:

28,929,716 (July 2014 est.)

country comparison to the world: 45

Age structure:

0-14 years: 24.9% (male 3,693,838/female 3,514,734)

15-24 years: 20.5% (male 3,008,779/female 2,934,534)

25-54 years: 43% (male 6,178,921/female 6,255,715)

55-64 years: 4.8% (male 926,129/female 1,036,576)

65 years and over: 4.7% (male 588,881/female 791,609) (2014 est.)

Median age:

total: 27.1 years

male: 26.6 years

female: 27.7 years (2014 est.)

Population growth rate:

0.93% (2014 est.)

country comparison to the world: 125

Birth rate:

17.02 births/1,000 population (2014 est.)

country comparison to the world: 109

Death rate:

5.29 deaths/1,000 population (2014 est.)

country comparison to the world: 181

Net migration rate:

-2.46 migrant(s)/1,000 population (2014 est.)

country comparison to the world: 173

Urbanization:

urban population: 36.2% of total population (2011)

rate of urbanization: 1.27% annual rate of change (2010-15 est.)

Major cities - population:

TASHKENT (capital) 2.201 million (2009)

Sex ratio:

at birth: 1.06 male(s)/female

under 15 years: 1.05 male(s)/female

15-24 years: 1.03 male(s)/female

25-54 years: 0.99 male(s)/female

55-64 years: 0.99 male(s)/female

65 years and over: 0.75 male(s)/female

total population: 0.99 male(s)/female (2014 est.)

Maternal mortality rate:

28 deaths/100,000 live births (2010)

country comparison to the world: 127

Infant mortality rate:

total: 19.84 deaths/1,000 live births

country comparison to the world: 91

male: 23.54 deaths/1,000 live births

female: 15.93 deaths/1,000 live births (2014 est.)

Life expectancy at birth:

total population: 73.29 years

country comparison to the world: 125

male: 70.25 years

female: 76.52 years (2014 est.)

Total fertility rate:

1.8 children born/woman (2014 est.)

country comparison to the world: 154

Health expenditures:

5.4% of GDP (2011)

country comparison to the world: 123

Physicians density:

2.54 physicians/1,000 population (2010)

Hospital bed density:

4.5 beds/1,000 population (2010)

Sanitation facility access:

improved:

urban: 100% of population

rural: 100% of population

total: 100% of population

unimproved:

urban: 0% of population

rural: 0% of population

total: 0% of population

HIV/AIDS - adult prevalence rate:

0.1% (2012)

country comparison to the world: 150

HIV/AIDS - people living with HIV/AIDS:

29,700 (2012)

country comparison to the world: 71

HIV/AIDS - deaths:

2,400 (2012)

country comparison to the world: 55

Children under the age of 5 years underweight:

4.4% (2006)

country comparison to the world: 97

Education expenditures:

NA

Literacy:

    definition: age 15 and over can read and write

    total population: 99.4%

    male: 99.6%

    female: 99.2% (2011 est.)

School life expectancy (primary to tertiary education):

    total: 12 years

    male: 12 years

    female: 11 years (2011)

Chapter 4: Government and Key Leaders

Country name:

conventional long form: Republic of Uzbekistan

conventional short form: Uzbekistan

local long form: O'zbekiston Respublikasi

local short form: O'zbekiston

former: Uzbek Soviet Socialist Republic

Government type:

republic; authoritarian presidential rule, with little power outside the executive branch

Capital:

name: Tashkent (Toshkent)

geographic coordinates: 41 19 N, 69 15 E

time difference: UTC+5 (10 hours ahead of Washington, DC during Standard Time)

Administrative divisions:

12 provinces (viloyatlar, singular - viloyat), 1 autonomous republic* (avtonom respublikasi), and 1 city** (shahar); Andijon Viloyati, Buxoro Viloyati, Farg'ona Viloyati, Jizzax Viloyati, Namangan Viloyati, Navoiy Viloyati, Qashqadaryo Viloyati (Qarshi), Qoraqalpog'iston Respublikasi [Karakalpakstan Republic]* (Nukus), Samarqand Viloyati, Sirdaryo Viloyati (Guliston), Surxondaryo Viloyati (Termiz), Toshkent Shahri [Tashkent City]**, Toshkent Viloyati [Tashkent province], Xorazm Viloyati (Urganch)

note: administrative divisions have the same names as their administrative centers (exceptions have the administrative center name following in parentheses)

Independence:

1 September 1991 (from the Soviet Union)

National holiday:

Independence Day, 1 September (1991)

Constitution:

several previous; latest adopted 8 December 1992; amended several times, last in 2012 (2012)

Legal system:

civil law system

International law organization participation:

has not submitted an ICJ jurisdiction declaration; non-party state to the ICCt

Suffrage:

18 years of age; universal

Executive branch:

chief of state: President Islom KARIMOV (since 24 March 1990, when he was elected president by the then Supreme Soviet; first elected president of independent Uzbekistan in 1991)

head of government: Prime Minister Shavkat MIRZIYOYEV (since 11 December 2003); First Deputy Prime Minister Rustam AZIMOV (since 2 January 2008)

cabinet: Cabinet of Ministers appointed by the president with approval of both chambers of the Supreme Assembly (Oliy Majlis)

elections: president elected by popular vote for a five-year term (eligible for a second term; previously was a five-year term, extended by a 2002 constitutional amendment to seven years and changed back to five years in 2011); election last held on 23 December 2007 (next to be held first quarter 2015); prime minister, ministers, and deputy ministers appointed by the president; note - to present a facade of democracy, the president nominates a candidate for prime minister, who then must be approved by a majority vote in both chambers of parliament

election results: Islom KARIMOV reelected president; percent of vote - Islom KARIMOV 88.1%, Asliddin RUSTAMOV 3.2%, Dilorom TOSHMUHAMEDOVA 2.9%, Akmal SAIDOV 2.6%, other 3.2%

Legislative branch:

bicameral Supreme Assembly or Oliy Majlis consists of an upper house or Senate (100 seats; 84 members elected by regional governing councils and 16 appointed by the president; members to serve five-year terms) and a lower house or Legislative Chamber (Qonunchilik Palatasi) (150 seats; 135 members elected by popular vote to serve five-year terms, while 15 spots reserved for the Ecological Movement of Uzbekistan)

elections: last held on 27 December 2009 and 10 January 2010 (next to be held in December 2014)

election results: Senate - percent of vote by party - NA; seats by party - NA; Legislative Chamber - percent of vote by party - NA; seats by party - LDPU 53, NDP 32, National Rebirth Party 31, Adolat 19

note: all parties in the Supreme Assembly support President Islom KARIMOV

Judicial branch:

highest court(s): Supreme Court (consists of 34 judges organized in civil, criminal, and military sections); Constitutional Court (consists of 7 judges); Higher Economic Court (consists of 19 judges) judge selection and term of office: judges of the 3 highest courts nominated by the president and confirmed by the Oliy Majlis; judges appointed for 5-year terms subject to reappointment

subordinate courts: regional, district, city, and town courts

Political parties and leaders:

Batkivshchyna (All-Ukrainian Union "Fatherland") [Yuliya TYMOSHENKO]
Communist Party of Ukraine or CPU [Petro SYMONENKO]
European Party of Ukraine [Mykola KATERYNCHUK]
Front of Change [Arseniy YATSENYUK]
Our Ukraine [Viktor YUSHCHENKO]
Party of Industrialists and Entrepreneurs [Anatoliy KINAKH]
Party of Regions [Mykola AZAROV, chairman]
Party of the Defenders of the Fatherland [Yuriy KARMAZIN]
People's Movement of Ukraine (Rukh) [Borys TARASYUK]
People's Party [Volodymyr LYTVYN]
Peoples' Self-Defense Party [Oleh NOVIKOV]
Progressive Socialist Party [Natalya VITRENKO]
Radical Party [Oleh LYASHKO]
Reforms and Order Party [Viktor PYNZENYK]
Republican Party Sobor [Anatoliy MATVIYENKO]
Social Democratic Party (United) or SDPU(o) [Yuriy ZAHORODNIY]
Socialist Party of Ukraine or SPU [Oleksandr MOROZ]
Svoboda [Oleh TYAHNYBOK]
Ukraine-Forward! [Natalia KOROLEVSKA]
Ukrainian Democratic Alliance for Reforms or UDAR [Vitaliy KLYCHKO]
Ukrainian People's Party [Yuriy KOSTENKO]
Union [Lev MIRIMSKY]
United Center [Viktor BALOHA]
Viche [Inna BOHOSLOVSKA]

Political pressure groups and leaders:

Committee of Voters of Ukraine [Aleksandr CHERNENKO]
OPORA [Olha AIVAZOVSKA]

International organization participation:

Australia Group, BSEC, CBSS (observer), CD, CE, CEI, CICA (observer), CIS (participating member, has not signed the 1993 CIS charter although it participates in meetings), EAEC (observer), EAPC, EBRD, FAO, GCTU, GUAM, IAEA, IBRD, ICAO, ICC (national committees), ICRM, IDA, IFC, IFRCS, IHO, ILO, IMF, IMO, IMSO, Interpol, IOC, IOM, IPU, ISO, ITU, ITUC (NGOs), LAIA (observer), MIGA, MONUSCO, NAM (observer), NSG, OAS (observer), OIF (observer), OPCW, OSCE, PCA, PFP, SELEC (observer), UN, UNCTAD,

UNESCO, UNIDO, UNMIL, UNMISS, UNWTO, UPU, WCO, WFTU (NGOs), WHO, WIPO, WMO, WTO, ZC

Diplomatic representation in the US:

chief of mission: Ambassador Oleksandr MOTSYK (since 24 June 2010)

chancery: 3350 M Street NW, Washington, DC 20007

telephone: [1] (202) 349-2920

FAX: [1] (202) 333-0817

Consulate(s) general: Chicago, New York, San Francisco

Diplomatic representation from the US:

chief of mission: Ambassador Geoffrey R. PYATT (since 30 July 2013)

embassy: 4 Igor Sikorsky Street, 04112 Kyiv

mailing address: 5850 Kyiv Place, Washington, DC 20521-5850

telephone: [380] (44) 521-5000

FAX: [380] (44) 521-5155

Key Leaders:

Pres.	Islom KARIMOV
Prime Min.	Shavkat MIRZIYOYEV
First Dep. Prime Min.	Rustam AZIMOV
Dep. Prime Min.	Elmira BASITHANOVA
Dep. Prime Min.	Gulomjon IBRAGIMOV
Dep. Prime Min.	Adham IKROMOV
Dep. Prime Min.	Ulugbek ROZIQULOV
Dep. Prime Min.	Botir ZOKIROV
Min. of Agriculture & Water Resources	Shuhrat TESHAYEV
Min. of Culture & Sports	Minhojiddin HOJIMATOV
Min. of Defense	Qobul BERDIYEV
Min. of Economics	Galina SAIDOVA
Min. of Emergency Situations	Tursunxon XUDOYBERGANOV
Min. of Finance	Rustam AZIMOV
Min. of Foreign Affairs	Abdulaziz KAMILOV
Min. of Foreign Economic Relations, Investments, & Trade	Elyor GANIYEV
Min. of Higher & Secondary Specialized Education	Baxodir XODIYEV
Min. of Internal Affairs	Adhamjon AHMADBOYEV
Min. of Justice	Nigmatilla YOLDOSHEV
Min. of Labor & Social Security	Aktam XAITOV
Min. of Public Education	Ulugbek INOYATOV
Min. of Public Health	Anvar ALIMOV
Sec., National Security Council	Viktor MAHMUDOV, *Lt. Gen.*
Chmn., National Security Service	Rustam INOYATOV, *Col. Gen.*
Chmn., State Bank	Fayzulla MULLAJANOV
Ambassador to the US	Baxtiyor GULOMOV

Flag description:

three equal horizontal bands of blue (top), white, and green separated by red fimbriations with a white crescent moon (closed side to the hoist) and 12 white stars shifted to the hoist on the top band; blue is the color of the Turkic peoples and of the sky, white signifies peace and the striving for purity in thoughts and deeds, while green represents nature and is the color of Islam; the red stripes are the vital force of all living organisms that links good and pure ideas with the eternal sky and with deeds on earth; the crescent represents Islam and the 12 stars the months and constellations of the Uzbek calendar

National symbol(s):

khumo (mythical bird)

National anthem:

name: "O'zbekiston Respublikasining Davlat Madhiyasi" (National Anthem of the Republic of Uzbekistan)

lyrics/music: Abdulla ARIPOV/Mutal BURHANOV

note: adopted 1992; after the fall of the Soviet Union, Uzbekistan kept the music of the anthem from its time as a Soviet Republic but adopted new lyrics

Chapter 5: Economy

Economy - overview:

Uzbekistan is a dry, landlocked country; 11% of the land is intensely cultivated, in irrigated river valleys. More than 60% of the population lives in densely populated rural communities. Export of hydrocarbons, primarily natural gas, provide a significant share of foreign exchange earnings. Other major export earners include gold and cotton. Despite ongoing efforts to diversify crops, Uzbekistani agriculture remains largely centered around cotton, although production has dropped by 35% since 1991. Uzbekistan is now the world's fifth largest cotton exporter and sixth largest producer. The country is aggressively addressing international criticism for the use of child labor in its cotton harvest. Following independence in September 1991, the government sought to prop up its Soviet-style command economy with subsidies and tight controls on production and prices. While aware of the need to improve the investment climate, the government still sponsors measures that often increase, not decrease, its control over business decisions. A sharp increase in the inequality of income distribution has hurt the lower ranks of society since independence. In 2003, the government accepted Article VIII obligations under the IMF, providing for full currency convertibility. However, strict currency controls and tightening of borders have lessened the effects of convertibility and have also led to some shortages that have further stifled economic activity. The Central Bank often delays or restricts convertibility, especially for consumer goods. Uzbekistan's growth has been driven primarily by state-led investments and a favorable export environment. In the past Uzbekistani authorities have accused US and other foreign companies operating in Uzbekistan of violating Uzbekistani tax laws and have frozen their assets. At the same time, the Uzbekistani Government has actively courted several major US and international corporations, offering attractive financing and tax advantages, and has landed a significant US investment in the automotive industry, including the opening of a powertrain manufacturing facility in Tashkent in November 2011. Uzbekistan has seen few effects from the global economic downturn, primarily due to its relative isolation from the global financial markets.

GDP (purchasing power parity):

$112.6 billion (2013 est.)

country comparison to the world: 70

$105.2 billion (2012 est.)

$97.21 billion (2011 est.)

note: data are in 2013 US dollars

GDP (official exchange rate):

$55.18 billion (2013 est.)

GDP - real growth rate:

7% (2013 est.)

8.2% (2012 est.)

8.3% (2011 est.)

GDP - per capita (PPP):

$3,800 (2013 est.)

country comparison to the world: 171

$3,600 (2012 est.)

$3,300 (2011 est.)

note: data are in 2013 US dollars

GDP - composition by sector:

agriculture: 19.1%

industry: 32.2%

services: 48.7% (2013 est.)

Labor force:

16.99 million (2013 est.)

country comparison to the world: 38

Labor force - by occupation:

agriculture: 25.9%

industry: 13.2%

services: 60.9% (2012 est.)

Unemployment rate:

4.9% (2013 est.)

country comparison to the world: 47

4.9% (2012 est.)

note: officially measured by the Ministry of Labor, plus another 20% underemployed

Population below poverty line:

17% (2011 est.)

Budget:

revenues: $17.84 billion

expenditures: $18.05 billion (2013 est.)

Taxes and other revenues:

32.3% of GDP (2013 est.)

country comparison to the world: 81

Budget surplus (+) or deficit (-):

-0.4% of GDP (2013 est.)

country comparison to the world: 52

Public debt:

7.6% of GDP (2013 est.)

country comparison to the world: 149

6.2% of GDP (2012 est.)

Inflation rate (consumer prices):

10.1% (2013 est.)

country comparison to the world: 209

11.4% (2012 est.)

Stock of narrow money:

$6.514 billion (31 December 2013 est.)

country comparison to the world: 93

$5.994 billion (31 December 2012 est.)

Stock of broad money:

$10.88 billion (31 December 2013 est.)

country comparison to the world: 103

$9.463 billion (31 December 2012 est.)

Stock of domestic credit:

$7.661 billion (31 December 2013 est.)

country comparison to the world: 106

$7.244 billion (31 December 2012 est.)

Current account balance:

$1.801 billion (2013 est.)

country comparison to the world: 44

$1.807 billion (2012 est.)

Exports:

$14.91 billion (2013 est.)

country comparison to the world: 80

$14.38 billion (2012 est.)

Exports - commodities:

energy products, cotton, gold, mineral fertilizers, ferrous and nonferrous metals, textiles, food products, machinery, automobiles

Exports - partners:

China 21.2%, Kazakhstan 15.9%, Turkey 15.8%, Russia 14.7%, Bangladesh 9.5%, Kyrgyzstan 4% (2012)

Imports:

$12.64 billion (2013 est.)

country comparison to the world: 90

$12.06 billion (2012 est.)

Imports - commodities:

machinery and equipment, foodstuffs, chemicals, ferrous and nonferrous metals

Imports - partners:

Russia 20.7%, China 16.6%, South Korea 16.4%, Kazakhstan 12.5%, Germany 4.6%, Turkey 4.2%, Ukraine 4% (2012)

Reserves of foreign exchange and gold:

$17 billion (31 December 2013 est.)

country comparison to the world: 64

$16 billion (31 December 2012 est.)

Debt - external:

$8.773 billion (31 December 2013 est.)

country comparison to the world: 103

$7.342 billion (31 December 2012 est.)

Exchange rates:

Uzbekistani soum (UZS) per US dollar -

2,082.3 (2013 est.)
1,890.1 (2012 est.)
1,587.2 (2010 est.)
1,466.7 (2009)
1,317 (2008)

Fiscal year:

calendar year

Chapter 6: Energy

Electricity - production:

    52.53 billion kWh (2012 est.)

    country comparison to the world: 50

Electricity - consumption:

    44.51 billion kWh (2010 est.)

    country comparison to the world: 51

Electricity - exports:

    12.09 billion kWh (2010 est.)

    country comparison to the world: 18

Electricity - imports:

    12 billion kWh (2010 est.)

    country comparison to the world: 16

Electricity - installed generating capacity:

    11.6 million kW (2010 est.)

    country comparison to the world: 51

Electricity - from fossil fuels:

    85.1% of total installed capacity (2010 est.)

    country comparison to the world: 88

Electricity - from nuclear fuels:

    0% of total installed capacity (2010 est.)

    country comparison to the world: 197

Electricity - from hydroelectric plants:

    14.9% of total installed capacity (2010 est.)

    country comparison to the world: 103

Electricity - from other renewable sources:

    0% of total installed capacity (2010 est.)

    country comparison to the world: 134

Crude oil - production:

    102,600 bbl/day (2012 est.)

    country comparison to the world: 49

Crude oil - exports:

0 bbl/day (2010 est.)

country comparison to the world: 200

Crude oil - imports:

0 bbl/day (2010 est.)

country comparison to the world: 135

Crude oil - proved reserves:

594 million bbl (1 January 2013 es)

country comparison to the world: 48

Refined petroleum products - production:

92,300 bbl/day (2010 est.)

country comparison to the world: 76

Refined petroleum products - consumption:

137,100 bbl/day (2011 est.)

country comparison to the world: 71

Refined petroleum products - exports:

4,968 bbl/day (2010 est.)

country comparison to the world: 90

Refined petroleum products - imports:

655.9 bbl/day (2010 est.)

country comparison to the world: 200

Natural gas - production:

62.9 billion cu m (2012 est.)

country comparison to the world: 13

Natural gas - consumption:

46.8 billion cu m (2012 est.)

country comparison to the world: 19

Natural gas - exports:

13.4 billion cu m (2012 est.)

country comparison to the world: 22

Natural gas - imports:

0 cu m (2012 est.)

country comparison to the world: 143

Natural gas - proved reserves:

1.841 trillion cu m (1 January 2013 es)

country comparison to the world: 20

Carbon dioxide emissions from consumption of energy:

115.9 million Mt (2011 est.)

country comparison to the world: 38

Chapter 7: Communications

Telephones - main lines in use:

1.963 million (2012)

country comparison to the world: 60

Telephones - mobile cellular:

20.274 million (2012)

country comparison to the world: 48

Telephone system:

general assessment: digital exchanges in large cities and in rural areas

domestic: the state-owned telecommunications company, Uzbektelecom, owner of the fixed line telecommunications system, has used loans from the Japanese government and the China Development Bank to upgrade fixed-line services including conversion to digital exchanges; mobile-cellular services are provided by 3 private and 1 state-owned operator with a total subscriber base of 19 million as of January 2014

international: country code - 998; linked by fiber-optic cable or microwave radio relay with CIS member states and to other countries by leased connection via the Moscow international gateway switch; the country also has a link to the Trans-Asia-Europe (TAE) fiber-optic cable; Uzbekistan has supported the national fiber optic backbone project of Afghanistan since 2008 (2009)

Broadcast media:

government controls media; 14 state-owned broadcasters - 10 TV and 4 radio - provide service to virtually the entire country; about 20 privately owned TV stations, overseen by local officials, broadcast to local markets; privately owned TV stations are required to lease transmitters from the government-owned Republic TV and Radio Industry Corporation; in 2013, the government closed TV and radio broadcasters affiliated with the National Association of Electronic Mass Media of Uzbekistan, a government-sponsored NGO for private broadcast media

Internet country code:

.uz

Internet hosts:

56,075 (2012)

country comparison to the world: 94

Internet users:

4.689 million (2009)

country comparison to the world: 50

Chapter 8: Transnational Issues

Disputes - international:

> prolonged drought and cotton monoculture in Uzbekistan and Turkmenistan created water-sharing difficulties for Amu Darya river states; field demarcation of the boundaries with Kazakhstan commenced in 2004; border delimitation of 130 km of border with Kyrgyzstan is hampered by serious disputes around enclaves and other areas

Refugees and internally displaced persons:

> IDPs: undetermined (government forcibly relocated an estimated 3,400 people from villages near the Tajikistan border in 2000-2001; no new data is available) (2012)

Trafficking in persons:

> current situation: Uzbekistan is a source country for men, women, and children subjected to forced labor and women and children subjected to sex trafficking; adults and children are victims of government-organized forced labor during Uzbekistan's annual cotton harvest; some Uzbekistani adults are subjected to forced labor in Kazakhstan, Russia, and, to a much lesser extent, Ukraine in domestic service, agriculture, and the construction and oil industries; Uzbekistani women and children, lured with fraudulent job offers, are sex trafficked to countries in Central Asia, the Middle East, Europe, and Asia; small numbers of Tajikistani and Kyrgyzstani victims have been identified in Uzbekistan

> tier rating: Tier 3 - Uzbekistan does not fully comply with the minimum standards for the elimination of trafficking and because it is not deemed to be making significant efforts to do so, it was downgraded to Tier 3 after the maximum of two consecutive annual waivers; the government has identified an increased number of sex and transnational labor trafficking victims; for the first time a decree was implemented banning the forced labor of children under the age of 15 in the annual cotton harvest, but government-organized forced labor of adults and older children contines in the cotton and reportedly other sectors; Uzbekistan does not have a systematic process to proactively identify trafficking victims and refer them to protective services (2013)

Illicit drugs:

> transit country for Afghan narcotics bound for Russian and, to a lesser extent, Western European markets; limited illicit cultivation of cannabis and small amounts of opium poppy for domestic consumption; poppy cultivation almost wiped out by government crop eradication program; transit point for heroin precursor chemicals bound for Afghanistan

Chapter 9: Transportation

Airports:

    53 (2013)

    country comparison to the world: 89

Airports - with paved runways:

    total: 33

    over 3,047 m: 6

    2,438 to 3,047 m: 13

    1,524 to 2,437 m: 6

    914 to 1,523 m: 4

    under 914 m: 4 (2013)

Airports - with unpaved runways:

    total: 20

    1,524 to 2,437 m: 2

    under 914 m: 18 (2013)

Pipelines:

    gas 10,401 km; oil 944 km (2013)

Railways:

    total: 4,230 km

    country comparison to the world: 40

    broad gauge: 4,200 km 1.520-m gauge (930 km electrified) (2012)

Roadways:

    total: 86,496 km

    country comparison to the world: 53

    paved: 75,511 km

    unpaved: 10,985 km (2000)

Waterways:

    1,100 km (2012)

    country comparison to the world: 63

Ports and terminals:

    river port(s): Termiz (Amu Darya)

Chapter 10: Military

Military branches:

Uzbek Armed Forces: Army, Air and Air Defense Forces (2013)

Military service age and obligation:

18 years of age for compulsory military service; 1-month or 1-year conscript service obligation for males; moving toward a professional military, but conscription in some form will continue; the military cannot accommodate everyone who wishes to enlist, and competition for entrance into the military is similar to the competition for admission to universities (2013)

Manpower available for military service:

males age 16-49: 7,887,292

females age 16-49: 7,886,459 (2010 est.)

Manpower fit for military service:

males age 16-49: 6,566,118

females age 16-49: 6,745,818 (2010 est.)

Manpower reaching militarily significant age annually:

male: 306,404

female: 295,456 (2010 est.)

Map of Uzbekistan

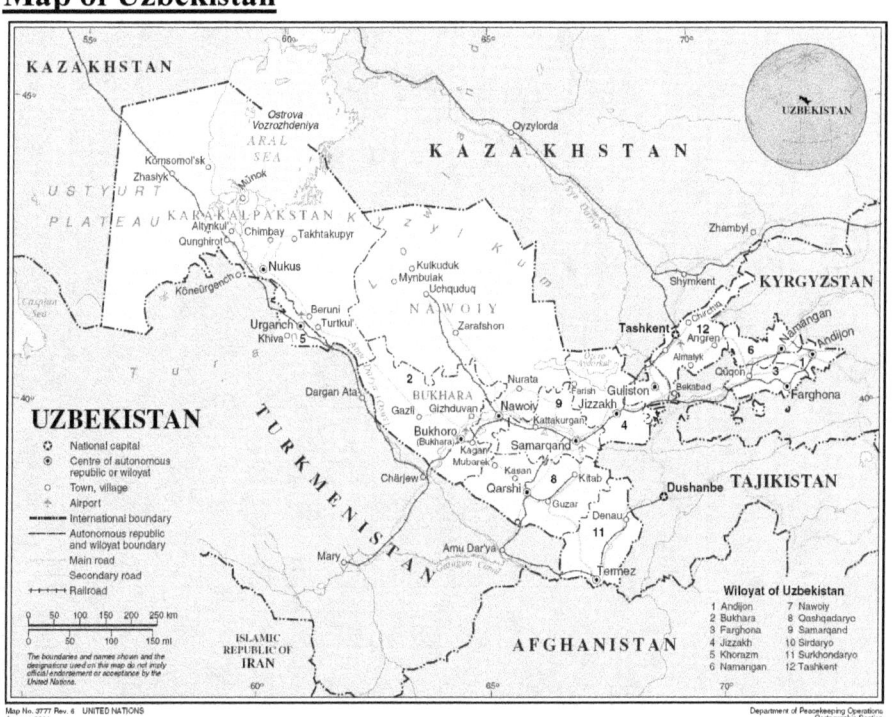

Other Key Facts™ Titles

All Key Facts™ Titles are Available at www.Amazon.com

THE INTERNATIONALIST®

2014

www.internationalist.com

www.ingramcontent.com/pod-product-compliance
Lightning Source LLC
Chambersburg PA
CBHW070733180526
45167CB00004B/1735